2X 10

# Wild Flowers of Massachusetts

## BY JOHN E. KLIMAS, JR.

WALKER AND COMPANY

NEW YORK

*To my good friend Dr. Sal Santella,*
*who spends many relaxing hours with his family*
*at Windy Hill farm in Massachusetts*

The publisher is grateful to
Roy and Margot Larsen and the Connecticut Audubon Society
who helped inspire the concept of this guide.

First published in the United States of America
in 1975 by the Walker Publishing Company, Inc.

Published simultaneously in Canada
by Fitzhenry & Whiteside, Limited, Toronto.

ISBN: 0-8027-0489-1

Library of Congress Catalog Card Number: 74-31929

Printed in the United States of America.

10    9    8    7    6    5    4    3    2    1

# Contents

# Introduction

IN the northeastern part of the United States, wild flowers form a colorful part of our natural environment for at least six months of the year. Because of their color, variety, and beauty, they generate a sense of curiosity that leads the amateur naturalist or casual hiker to want to learn more about them. The purpose of this book is to enable one who has had no previous botanical training to identify some of the most common wild flowers found in Massachusetts and surrounding states. It contains a selection of photographs and commentary on those wild flowers that, because of color, size, or number, are most likely to catch one's eye.

## Names of Wild Flowers

All flowers are listed under their common names and scientific names (genus and species), along with their family affiliations. This nomenclature conforms with that found in the eighth edition of *Gray's Manual of Botany*. The common names of wild flowers are given because many of them are steeped in lore and history that gives a special significance to the flower you might find. The scientific names are also given to avoid the confusion that often results from giving only the common names. Some wild flowers have more than one common name, while the common name of others will vary from region to region or even within a single region. I have endeavored to make the learning of both common and scientific names easy and interesting by explaining their derivations. But don't let learning the names of wild flowers deter you from enjoying their beauty and grace. As Shakespeare said, ". . . a rose by any other name would smell as sweet."

## Lore and Uses of Wild Flowers

Learning to recognize wild flowers is only half the fun of this type of activity. Many wild flowers have folklore and legends associated with them that make them more than just a collection of petals, stems, and leaves. Many of the common names of plants are derived from the "doctrine of signatures," an antiquated theory used by herb doctors and Indian medicine men that stated that the outward appearance of a plant indicated its special properties, which could be used in magic or healing. Thus, for example, a medicine prepared from *Hepatica* (commonly called 'Liverleaf') was used to treat liver ailments because the shape of the leaf was thought to resemble the human liver. Although in some cases a plant was later found to contain a substance that had medicinal value, the success claimed for many plants used in early medicine was equivalent to our modern-day placebo—the sugar-coated pill. A placebo, accompanied by a kind word and the sympathetic ear of a doctor in which a sick person has great faith, can often work wonders!

Wild flowering plants also had other uses. Some contain a colored juice in their stems or roots or fruit that were used as dyes. Parts of wild flowering plants were used as foods by early Americans. A list of the edible parts of plants described in this book is found on page 8.

### When and Where to Look for Wild Flowers

In the spring we look for the first flowers in the woods. They are given a head start by the warmth of the natural mulch of fallen leaves; and, since most sprout from bulbs or tubers, there is no waiting for the germination of seeds. Most spring flowers are short-lived. Toward the end of May and the beginning of June we see a lesser number of flowers in the woods because the trees have developed their foliage and shade prevents the growth of all but shade-tolerant plants. The place to look for wild flowers at this time is in the open woods or in the meadows. Many of these plants continue to bloom until the fall.

Many areas of Massachusetts are covered by an urban sprawl, but this should not discourage one from studying wild flowers. In the city many wild flowers are found growing in parks, vacant lots, alongside highways, and even around the city dump. One of the most prolific areas for finding wild flowers in an urban area is along a railroad right-of-way. Many unique kinds of plants not found elsewhere in the state are found in the marshes and bogs along the coast of Massachusetts and especially Cape Cod. Several areas throughout Massachusetts have been set aside as sanctuaries and nature centers where wild flowers are not only protected but in most cases trails and self-guided tours make them readily accessible for viewing and identification. These are listed on pages 4–6, including a map designating their locations. On page 7 there is also a listing of wild flowers in the types of habitat in which they are most likely to be found.

### Cultivating and Propagating Wild Flowers

Wild flowers add that color and zest to a landscape that would otherwise be rather dull. In an effort to bring some of this natural charm into the home garden, people attempt to cultivate and propagate wild flowers. This is often difficult to do since the casual-appearing requirements for the growth of wild flowers are actually fairly stringent. One must not only consider the location of the garden but also such factors as type of soil, moisture, amount of light, and other conditions. Many wild flowers can be successfully transplanted if large enough pieces of sod are taken along with the plant. If plants have deep tap roots, they cannot be transplanted in the adult stage but can be successfully transplanted as seedlings. Some wild flowers are annuals or biennials and are best brought to your garden as seeds.

Specific methods of propagation for each of the wild flowers in this book are contained in the text with the designation: *S = seeds, R = bulb or root division, C = cutting*. For detailed information on the cultivation of wild flowers, see: Taylor, Kathryn S., and Hamblin, Stephen F., *Handbook of Wild Flower Cultivation*. New York: Macmillan Publishing Co., 1962.

A FINAL NOTE: wild flowers on the Protected List of the Garden Club of America and the New England Wild Flower Society are designated with the symbol †appearing after names in the text. No attempt should be made to transplant or cultivate these plants unless they are in danger of being destroyed by highway construction or building developments.

## How to Use This Book

To avoid baffling or discouraging the beginner, this elementary guidebook minimizes the technical jargon of the botanist and uses color as the key to identification. Although color has its limitations, it serves the beginner well. Not only are the flowers arranged by color, but also flowers of the same color are arranged by the seasons in which they usually appear. There is also a season and color listing of the flowers on page 57.

When you have found a flower you would like to identify, observe the predominant coloration. Check through that section of the book containing the photographs of flowers of that coloration. Sometimes it is difficult to determine the color of a flower, especially since blues, purples, and pinks gradually blend one into the other. In this case make a decision for one color and if the flower is not identified, try another color section that might include it. Once you have found what you believe is the correct flower, refer to the written description of each flower. This text contains other botanical features—such as size of flower; height of plant; habitat; and characteristics of fruit, foliage, and stem—that will help to confirm your identification. Because of the large number of species in some genera, the particular species you may have found might not be illustrated, but at least you will know what kind of a flower it is. The section "Similar Plants" describes additional plants that are similar to ones pictured and described in the main text.

Also remember that you might find a fairly rare or relatively inconspicuous wild flower that is not described in this guide. The following works can be used in these identifications and for additional information: Rickett, Harold W., *Wild Flowers of the United States: The Northeastern States*, 2 vols. New York, McGraw-Hill Book Company, 1966; and Klimas, John E., and Cunningham, James, *Wildflowers of Eastern America*, New York: Alfred A. Knopf, 1974.

# Massachusetts

## Nature Centers

---

### Barre
Wildwood Nature Center, South Street 01005. 40 acres. Guided and self-guided tours. Open all year.

### Brewster
Cape Cod Museum of Natural History (Route 6A) 02631. 60 acres. Self-guided tours. Open all year; closed Mondays and Fridays from October–May.

### Easthampton
Arcadia Nature Center and Wildlife Sanctuary 01027. 600 acres. Guided and self-guided tours. Open all year.

### Edgartown
Felix Neck Wildlife Sanctuary. Mailing address: Felix Neck Wildlife Trust, P.O. Box 494, Vineyard Haven, Massachusetts 02568. 200 acres. Guided and self-guided tours. Open all year.

### Hampden
Laughing Brook Education Center & Wildlife Sanctuary, 789 Main Street 01036. 100 acres. Guided and self-guided tours. Open all year; closed Mondays and holidays.

### Lenox
Pleasant Valley Wildlife Sanctuary 01240. 655 acres. Guided and self-guided tours. Special feature: active beaver colony. Open all year.

### Lincoln
Drumlin Farm Educational Center and Wildlife Sanctuary, South Great Road 01773. 240 acres. Guided and self-guided tours. Open all year; closed Mondays except Monday holidays.

### Milton
Blue Hills Trailside Museum, 1904 Canton Avenue 02186. 5,700 acres. Open all year, Monday holidays; closed Mondays, Thanksgiving, Christmas, and New Year's Day.

### Norfolk
Stony Brook Nature Center, North Street 02056. 200 acres. Self-guided tours. Open all year.

### Princeton
Wachusett Meadows Wildlife Sanctuary, Goodnow Road 01541. 960 acres, contains 100-acre marsh. Guided and self-guided tours. Open all year.

### Sharon
Moosehill Wildlife Sanctuary, 300 Moose Hill Street 02067. 260 acres. Self-guided tours. Open all year.

### South Wellfleet
Wellfleet Bay Wildlife Sanctuary, West Road, P.O. Box 236 02663. 650 acres. Self-guided tours. Open all year.

### Spencer
Buck Hill Conservation and Education Center, McCormick Road 01562. 300 acres. Guided and self-guided tours. Open all year.

### Topsfield
Ipswich River Nature Center and Wildlife Sanctuary 01983. 2,400 acres. Guided and self-guided tours. Open all year.

### Westwood
Hale Reservation, 80 Carby Street 02090. 1,000 acres. Guided and self-guided tours. Open all year.

# Habitats

### Wetlands

Arrowhead
Turtlehead
Jack-in-the-Pulpit
Cardinal Flower
Touch-me-not

Marsh Marigold
Yellow Loosestrife
Forget-me-not
Square-stem Monkey Flower

Swamp Mallow
Skunk Cabbage
Pickerelweed
Great Lobelia

### Woodlands

Trailing Arbutus
Wood Anemone
Rue Anemone
Dwarf Ginseng
Bloodroot
Dutchman's Breeches
White Trillium
Saxifrage
Spring Beauty
Wild Lily-of-the-Valley
Solomon's Seal

False Solomon's Seal
White Baneberry
Maystar
Wild Sarsaparilla
Mayapple
Spotted Wintergreen
Partridge Berry
Indian Pipes
Rattlesnake Plantain
White Woodland Aster
Cucumber Root

Red Trillium
Wild Columbine
Wood Lily
Golden Ragwort
Trout Lily
Lady Slipper
Wild Geranium
Liverleaf
Violet
Wood Betony

### Fields and Roadsides

Wild Strawberry
Daisy
Yarrow
Fleabane
Queen Anne's Lace
Horse Nettle
Tall Meadow Rue
Meadowsweet
Pearly Everlasting
Pokeweed
Boneset
Heath Aster
Butterfly Weed
Hawkweed
Coltsfoot
Celandine
Cinquefoil

Dandelion
Goldstar Grass
Buttercup
Butter and Eggs
Black-eyed Susan
St. Johnswort
Common Mullein
Evening Primrose
Partridge Pea
Wild Lettuce
Goldenrod
Wild Sunflower
Blue-eyed Grass
Dayflower
Blue Vervain
Chicory
Fringed Gentian

Star Thistle
Clover
Deptford Pink
Steeplebush
Meadow Beauty
Tick Trefoils
Cow Vetch
Bittersweet Nightshade
Virginia Spiderwort
Milkweed
Purple Milkwort
Heal-all
Bull Thistle
Joe-Pye-weed
Ironweed
New England Aster

# Edible Plant Parts

Edible plant parts discussed are those from plants not on the protected list, with the exception of those few protected plants that produce an edible fruit. Only the plant parts specified are edible and only when properly prepared. Specific directions and recipes for their preparation can be found in Adrienne Crowhurst's *The Weed Cookbook* (New York: Lancer Books, 1972).

## Leaves and Stems

SALAD GREENS (use tender, young leaves; these greens can also be cooked)

Dandelion
Wild Lettuce
Dayflower
Chicory

Clover
Meadow Beauty
Virginia Spiderwort

Violet (leaves only from plants with violet-colored flowers)
Pickerelweed (young, unfurled leaves)

COOKED GREENS (usually boiled with several changes of water)

Solomon's Seal
False Solomon's Seal
Pokeweed (young shoots only; mature stems with reddish tinge are poisonous)
Evening Primrose

Touch-me-not (young shoots)
Skunk Cabbage (young, unfurled leaves)
Milkweed (young shoots)

TEAS   Yarrow (use fresh leaves)

## Roots or Bulbs

RAW   Wild Sarsaparilla                                 Cucumber Root
(small quantities of chopped roots added to salad)

BOILED

Spring Beauty
Solomon's Seal

Queen Anne's Lace
Dandelion

Evening Primrose

ROASTED (after roasting, pulverize and use as a substitute for coffee)

Dandelion                          Partridge Pea                          Chicory

## Fruit, Pods, and Seeds

False Solomon's Seal: red berry (eat in moderation)
Wild Strawberry: red berry
Mayapple: yellow fruit

Partridge Berry: red berry
Wild Sunflower: seeds
Milkweed: young pods less than 1 inch long (eaten raw or boiled)

## Flowers

Dandelion (boil unopened flower buds)
Violet (fresh flowers of violet-colored species as salad garnish)

Milkweed (unopened flower heads cooked and served like broccoli)
Clover (dried flower heads used to make a tea)

8

KEY TO SYMBOLS: *The following letters indicate means of propagation*

$S = by\ seed$ $R = by\ bulb\ or\ root\ division$ $C = by\ taking\ cuttings$
† = flowers on protected list

# 1. *White Flowers*

---

**W-1** TRAILING ARBUTUS *(Epigaea repens)* † Heath family
*SRC* Height: Prostrate. Flower: ½″ diameter.
Season: Early spring (p.21)

This prostrate perennial with thick, oval-shaped, evergreen leaves is usually found in shaded woods on rocky, well-drained banks. Because of the shape and color of the leaves, this plant is often called "ground laurel." The delicate white blossoms, which appear in early spring, are produced at the ends of the branches and are extremely fragrant. Unfortunately, the trailing arbutus is becoming rare in this part of the country. This is rather ironic, since another name for the plant is "mayflower," because it was believed to have been the first flower the Pilgrims saw after their initial harsh winter in New England.

**W-2** WOOD ANEMONE *(Anemone quinquefolia)* † Buttercup family
*SR* Height: 8″–10″. Flower: 1″ diameter.
Season: Early spring (p.21)

The wood anemone is a small plant found in open woods in moderately rich soil. The more basal leaves are divided into five-pointed leaflets. The four to seven white "petals" are petal-like sepals. Because of their slender stems, the solitary flower trembles in the slightest breeze; hence the common name, "windflower." In ancient times it was believed that the wind that passed over a field of anenomes was poisoned and would cause sickness in anyone inhaling this air. This is perhaps the reason that the Persians adopted this flower as their emblem of illness.

**W-3** RUE ANEMONE *(Anemonella thalictroides)* † Buttercup family
*SR* Height: 4″–8″. Flower: ¾″ diameter.
Season: Early spring (p.21)

This plant is often confused with the wood anemone because they are found in the same habitat. The white flower is also composed of five to ten sepals. However, the rue anemone produces a cluster of flowers instead of a solitary blossom, and the leaves are divided into three round-lobed leaflets.

**W-4**    DWARF GINSENG *(Panax trifolius)*      Ginseng family
*SR*    Height: 3″–6″. Flower: ⅛″ diameter; 15–25 in spherical cluster.
     Season: Early spring                                       (p.21)

This low-growing herb is found along streams or in damp depressions in the woods. The leaves are composed of three or five leaflets. The underground stem, or tuber, is edible and pungent-tasting. For this reason the plant is often called groundnut.

**W-5**    BLOODROOT *(Sanguinaria canadensis)* †      Poppy family
*SR*    Height: 6″–10″. Flower: 1″–1½″ diameter.
     Season: Early spring                                         (p.21)

This short-lived flower is unusual because of the waxy, white color of its eight to twelve petals. The single leaf, heart-shaped with five to nine prominent lobes, is wrapped around the flower bud as it emerges from the ground; it expands only after the flower has bloomed. The plant is often found growing in clusters on shaded banks in rich woods. The rootstock and stem contain a bright-red, poisonous sap, to which the common name refers. It is said that the Indians used the sap not only as a dye for their garments and handiwork but also as a war paint when necessary.

**W-6**    DUTCHMAN'S BREECHES *(Dicentra cucullaria)*† Fumitory family
*SR*    Height: 6″–10″. Flower: ¾″ long.
     Season: Early spring                                         (p.21)

This plant is best found growing in clusters on rocky ledges. The common name is derived from the four to twelve two-spurred flowers on an arched stem that look like white pantaloons on a clothesline, hung with the yellow-belted waist down and the ankles up. The basal leaves are finely divided and fernlike.

**W-7**    WHITE TRILLIUM *(Trillium grandiflorum)* †      Lily family
*SR*    Height: 8″–14″. Flower: 3″–4″ diameter.
     Season: Early spring                                         (p.22)

Trilliums are characterized by having three leaves, three sepals, and three petals. The white trillium is one of the most striking of early spring flowers because of its large size. Although the flower is white when it first appears, the petals gradually change in color, so that after a time they become pink or dull rose. Look for these flowers on wooded slopes in rich woods.

**W-8**    SAXIFRAGE *(Saxifraga virginiensis)*                 Saxifrage family
*SR*       Height: 8″–15″. Flower: ¼″ long; branching cluster.
           Season: Early spring                                    (p.22)

The crevices of rocky cliffs and hillsides are the preferred habitat of this plant. The hairy, leafless stem bearing the flowers near the top springs from a basal rosette of paddle-shaped leaves. Saxifrage is a combination of two Latin words meaning "stone breaker," an obvious reference to its supposed ability to disintegrate the rock upon which it is growing. Observing this, herb doctors believed that the root of this plant could be used as a medicine to disintegrate kidney stones.

**W-9**    SPRING BEAUTY *(Claytonia virginica)*                Portulaca family
*SR*       Height: 4″–8″. Flower: ¾″ diameter.
           Season: Early spring                                    (p.22)

These delicate harbingers of spring grow in such large masses in open woods or meadows that they look like patches of unmelted snow. However, the five-petaled flowers with pink veins open only in bright sunlight, so they are not seen on cloudy days. The two grasslike leaves rise from a starchy bulb that was eaten by the Indians.

**W-10**   WILD LILY-OF-THE-VALLEY *(Maianthemum canadense)*
*S*        Height: 4″–6″. Flower: ¼″ diameter; 15–25 in a cluster.   Lily family
           Season: Spring                                          (p.22)

This plant is first seen as widespread patches of pointed, oval leaves on zigzag stems covering the floor of cool, moist woods. The stalk of white flowers appears in May; during the summer small clusters of speckled pale-red berries are produced. This plant is also called "Canada mayflower," since it grows in mass profusion in the Canadian woodlands.

**W-11**   SOLOMON'S SEAL *(Polygonatum pubescens)*              Lily family
*SR*       Height: 1′–2′. Flower: ½″ long.
           Season: Spring                                          (p.22)

These plants are common wherever there is a moist slope in open woods. The common name comes from the shape of the scar left by each previous year's stalk on the underground stem, which resembles the seal impressed in wax on official documents in former times. The arched stem has alternating lance-shaped leaves. The small, green-white, bell-shaped flowers originate from the base of each leaf and hang down singly or in pairs along the stem. During the summer dark-blue berries develop.  †

**W-12**    FALSE SOLOMON'S SEAL *(Smilacina racemosa)*    Lily family
*SR*      Height: 2′–3′. Flower: ¼″ diameter; terminal cluster.
       Season: Spring                    (p.22)

This plant resembles the true Solomon's Seal in general shape and habitat. It differs in that the arched stem is zigzag in shape and the white flowers are found in a showy cluster at the end of the stem. In the fall the flower cluster becomes a mass of red berries, which are quite conspicuous even in the colorful woods.

**W-13**    WILD STRAWBERRY *(Fragaria virginiana)*    Rose family
*C*      Height: Prostrate. Flower: ½″ diameter.
       Season: Spring                    (p.23)

Wild strawberry resembles the cultivated strawberry in being a creeping vine with leaves of three dark-green leaflets with coarse margins and white, five-petaled flowers. However, the fruit is much smaller than that obtained from the cultivated plant but is far superior in taste. This plant is found in rather dry soil in fields and on hillsides.

**W-14**    WHITE BANEBERRY *(Actaea pachypoda)*    Buttercup family
*SR*      Height: 1′–2′. Flower: ¼″ diameter; terminal cluster.
       Season: Spring                    (p.23)

In the open woods we seldom notice the baneberry, not because it is that rare a plant but because its flower cluster is rather inconspicuous above the main mass of sharp-toothed leaflets of the compound leaves. However, when the fruit ripens in the late summer, this is an eyecatching cluster of white, oval, berrylike fruit with a black tip; hence the common name "doll's eyes." These berries are poisonous, which accounts for the name "baneberry."

**W-15**    MAYSTAR *(Trientalis borealis)*    Primrose family
*S*      Height: 5″–7″. Flower: ½″ diameter.
       Season: Spring                    (p.23)

Cool, hilly woods are the optimum habitat for this plant. The white starflower, as it is often called, is star-shaped, with five to nine pointed petals found above a whorl of six to eight taper-pointed leaves.

**W-16**    WILD SARSAPARILLA *(Aralia nudicaulis)*    Ginseng family
*SR*      Height: 12″–15″. Flower: ¼″ diameter; spherical cluster.
       Season: Spring                    (p.23)

The roots of this plant are aromatic and were often used as a substitute for true sarsaparilla flavoring. The round clusters of greenish-white flowers are rather inconspicuous beneath the single leaf, which is divided into three compound leaflets. Look for this plant in rich, open woods.

**W-17**  DAISY *(Chrysanthemum leucanthemum)*  Composite family
*SR*  Height: 2′–3′. Flower: 1½″ diameter.
Season: Spring  (p.23)

This is a native of Europe that escaped cultivation when brought to this country. It is a member of the large composite family, characterized by each single flower actually being a grouping of many small flowers of two kinds—ray flowers and disk flowers. The mass of small disk flowers makes up the yellow center, which is surrounded by the petal-like white ray flowers. It is indeed a joyful sight to see a field of daisies, but farmers and dairymen find them a nuisance, since they are difficult to eradicate and ruin good pastureland.

**W-18**  YARROW *(Achillea millefolium)*  Composite family
*SR*  Height: 1′–2′. Flower: ¼″ diameter; flat-head cluster.
Season: Spring  (p.23)

A common roadside plant, the yarrow thrives in dry soil. Although the flower is not very attractive, the alternate leaves are finely dissected and feathery in appearance and the plant is often mistaken for a fern. Yarrow is a European perennial that escaped cultivation when it was brought to this country for its supposed medicinal value: the aromatic leaves were chewed as a remedy for toothache.

**W-19**  FLEABANE *(Erigeron spp.)*  Composite family
*SR*  Height: 2′–3′. Flower: 1″ diameter.
Season: Spring  (p.24)

The fleabanes are a weed of the open field and are usually found along with daisies, which they resemble in miniature. However, the ray flowers may range in color from white to lavender, and the narrow, elliptical leaves are without stalks and are attached directly to the hairy stem. The common name of these plants is derived from the belief that when dried and burned they would be a good insect repellent. Also plants were hung in country cottages for this reason.

**W-20**  MAYAPPLE *(Podophyllum peltatum)* †  Barberry family
*SR*  Height: 1′–1½′. Flower: 1″–1½″ diameter; nodding.
Season: Spring  (p.24)

The plant, which grows in dense patches in open woods, produces two fan-shaped leaves which hang in a horizontal position; hence its other common name, "umbrella leaf." A single, nodding, white, waxy flower is produced in the fork formed by the two leaf stalks. In the summer the "apple," which is really a juicy yellow berry, ripens. Another common name is "mandrake," but it is not related to the European mandrake, once much sought after because of its reputed magic properties.

**W-21** SPOTTED WINTERGREEN *(Chimaphila maculata)* †
C     Height: 4″–6″. Flower: ¾″ diameter; nodding.     Wintergreen family
      Season: Early summer                                    (p.24)

While most flowers are blooming in the sunny fields and meadows, a walk in the dark dry woods in July will be rewarded with the sight of clusters of small white flowers nodding above leathery, dark-green, white-striped leaves. Another common name for this plant is of Indian origin—"pipsissewa."

**W-22** PARTRIDGE BERRY *(Mitchella repens)* †          Madder family
SRC    Height: Prostrate. Flower: ¼″ diameter; pairs.
       Season: Early summer                                   (p.24)

This small, creeping evergreen with small, dark-green, oval leaves is found in the densely shaded parts of the woods, where it may form a thick mat. The white flowers occur in pairs, joined at their bases so that the single red berry formed later in the summer is actually two fused fruits. Because it can tolerate shade, is easily transplanted, and is evergreen, it is a much-used plant in indoor terrariums.

**W-23** QUEEN ANNE'S LACE *(Daucus carota)*          Carrot family
C      Height: 1′–3′. Flower: ⅛″ diameter; flat-head cluster.
       Season: Early summer                                   (p.24)

Another European immigrant, this plant closely resembles yarrow in appearance and habitat. The common name originated when someone in England decided the blossoms resembled Queen Anne's lace headdress. The leaves are feathery, and if you look closely at the center of the flower cluster, you will notice that one of the small flowers is dark purple. This plant had economic value, since it is the wild plant from which early man developed the common garden carrot. Crush a leaf between your fingers and note the odor of carrot.

**W-24** HORSE NETTLE *(Solanum carolinense)*          Nightshade family
S      Height: Sprawling vine. Flower: ¾″ diameter.
       Season: Early summer                                   (p.24)

This plant is found in sandy soil in meadows and fields. Although the plant is not a member of the rose family, the stems, branches, and even the underside of the deeply lobed, lance-shaped leaves are covered with prickles. The star-shaped flower produces bright-yellow berries in the fall.

**W-25**    TALL MEADOW RUE *(Thalictrum polygamum)*    Buttercup family
*SR*      Height: 3′–11′. Flower: ¼″ long; terminal cluster.
       Season: Summer                                        (p.25)

The tall, white, feathery clusters of flowers in wet meadows call our attention to this plant. A close look at the flowers, however, reveals that there are no petals and that the attractive tassels are composed of numerous white stamens. The feathery appearance of the plant is enhanced by the finely divided compound leaves, which are bluntly lobed.

**W-26**    MEADOWSWEET *(Spiraea latifolia)*            Rose family
*R*      Height: 2′–5′. Flower: ¼″ diameter; dense terminal cluster.
       Season: Summer                                         (p.25)

The normal habitat for this woody shrub is the moist meadow or wooded field. The distinguishing feature of this meadow plant is smooth, reddish stems, and branches with dark-green, oval, sparsely toothed leaves topped by the dense cluster of small white flowers.

**W-27**    PEARLY EVERLASTING *(Anaphalis margaritacea)*
                                                  Composite family
*SR*      Height: 1′–2′. Flower: ½″ diameter; terminal cluster.
       Season: Summer                                         (p.25)

Another plant found in dry, open fields is the white, woolly pearly everlasting. What appears to be a flower with a yellow center and white petals is actually a cluster of minute yellow flowers surrounded by numerous pearly-white scales (bracts). The common name, "everlasting," comes from the observation that although the stem and thin, lance-shaped leaves are green, they are covered with so much woolly material that they look like dead, preserved plants. If you crush a leaf between your fingers, it will emit a slight lemon scent.

**W-28**    INDIAN PIPES *(Monotropa uniflora)* †           Heath family
*S*      Height: 4″–8″. Flower: ½″ diameter; nodding.
       Season: Summer                                         (p.25)

The more rain that falls during the summer, the more often we can find this plant in the rich woods. Because it lacks chlorophyll, all parts of the plant—stems, leaves, and single, nodding flower—are white. Without chlorophyll to synthesize its food, it obtains nourishment from fungi that live in the soil. Because of its unusual waxy-white appearance, it is often picked. However, it soon turns black when picked, which accounts for its Indian name, "corpse plant."

**W-29**  POKEWEED *(Phytolacca americana)*  Poke family
S  Height: 3′–10′. Flower: ⅜″ diameter.
  Season: Summer  (p.25)

The flowers and berries are found at the same time on the same stalk on this plant.
Actually, the flower is devoid of petals but has five white sepals. A common
plant of fallow fields and waste places, the succulent purple stems and green,
lance-shaped leaves are poisonous when eaten by man or cattle. The clusters of
dark berries that develop are also poisonous, but they have found some use as a
primitive dye and at one time an alcohol solution of the juices was used as a treatment for rheumatism. Twigs of the plant were worn as campaign emblems by the
followers of President Polk, even though the names are spelled differently.

**W-30**  ARROWHEAD *(Sagittaria latifolia)* †  Arrowhead family
SR  Height: 1′–2′. Flower: 1″ diameter.
  Season: Summer  (p.25)

The peculiar arrow-shaped leaf is the reason for the common and scientific names
(*Sagitta* is Latin for "arrow") for this aquatic plant that is found along ponds and
the margins of sluggish streams. The conspicuous male flowers grow in whorls
of three along a common stalk, with the whorl of three inconspicuous female
flowers below. The stout underground stem of this plant not only provides a
source of food for many types of waterfowl; because of its high starch content,
it was used as a food source by the Algonquin Indians, and the men in the Lewis
and Clark expedition used it as a substitute for bread.

**W-31**  RATTLESNAKE PLANTAIN *(Goodyera pubescens)* † Orchid family
RC  Height: 6″–12″. Flower: ¼″ long; spikelike cluster.
  Season: Summer  (p.26)

A fairly rare member of the orchid family, this plant is found blooming in dry
woods in the summer. The common name is derived from the basal oval leaves
with their network of white lines. They were thought to resemble snakeskin and
therefore were supposed to be effective against snakebite if chewed or applied to
the bite. In fact, the Indian had such faith in their curative powers that he would
allow a poisonous snake to bite him for a sum of money if he had some leaves
available for medicinal purposes. Because of the attractive basal leaves and the
fact that the plant is easy to transplant, it is often used in terrariums.

**W-32** BONESET *(Eupatorium perfoliatum)*       Composite family
*S*      Height: 2′–5′. Flower: ¼″ diameter; flat-head cluster.
      Season: Late summer                        (p.26)

The unusual feature of this plant is the way the hairy stem seems to grow through the opposite, lance-shaped leaves that are united at their bases so that they surround the stem. Hence the specific name *perfoliatum*, Latin for "through the leaf." This unique characteristic is also responsible for the common name "boneset," since herb doctors believed that plants with united leaves could aid in uniting broken or fractured bones. Look for the flat-headed cluster of white flowers in moist meadows in the late summer, along with the goldenrods and Joe-Pye-weeds.

**W-33** WHITE WOODLAND ASTER *(Aster divaricatus)*
*SR*      Height: 2′–3′. Flower: ¾″ diameter.       Composite family
      Season: Late summer                        (p.26)

The asters are a large and difficult group to identify; only a few of the more common species are described in this book. Although most asters appear in meadows and along the edges of woods in the fall, this white aster blooms in the shaded woods in late summer. It is distinguished by its dark-brown or purple zigzag stem and sharply toothed, lance-shaped, dark-veined leaves.

**W-34** HEATH ASTER *(Aster ericoides)*       Composite family
*R*      Height: 1′–4′. Flower: ½″ diameter.
      Season: Late summer                        (p.26)

This white aster is found on the borders of dry fields. The plant is easily recognized because it has a bushy appearance and the small, stiff, crowded leaves are covered with minute gray hairs. If you see a grayish bush covered with numerous small white flowers in the late summer, you have found the heath aster.

**W-35** TURTLEHEAD *(Chelone glabra)* †       Figwort family
*SRC*      Height: 2′–5′. Flower: 1″–1½″ long; terminal cluster.
      Season: Late summer                        (p.26)

This plant thrives in wet, open woods and along streams. The generic name, *Chelone*, is the Greek word for "tortoise." The white, two-lipped flowers, resembling the head of a turtle, are clustered at the end of a single stalk with opposite, sharp-toothed, lance-shaped leaves. An ointment to relieve itching has been made from these leaves.

# 2. Green Flowers

---

**G-1**   JACK-IN-THE-PULPIT *(Arisaema triphyllum)* †          Arum family
*SR*      Height: 1′–2′. Flower: Inconspicuous; within spathe.
          Season: Spring                                        (p.26)

A favorite of children, this spring flower is a member of the same family as the earlier blooming skunk cabbage. The tall green "pulpit" (spathe) is streaked with purple or brown and arches over "Jack" (spadix), contained within it. The small, inconspicuous flowers, which may be male and/or female, are found clustered at "Jack's" feet. When one walks through the damp woodland habitat of this plant, the flower may be hidden by the one or two long-stalked leaves, divided into three leaflets. However, during the late summer, with the leaves dead, the flower is replaced by a glossy red fruit.

**G-2**   CUCUMBER ROOT *(Medeola virginiana)*                  Lily family
*S*       Height: 1′–2′. Flower: ⅜″ diameter.
          Season: Spring                                        (p.27)

Because the flowers are small and green, the plant itself is often recognized before the flower. The long slender stem has two whorls of leaves; the upper whorl usually has three narrow leaves and the lower whorl five to nine larger leaves. The small flower, found on long stalks above the upper whorl of leaves, has small green petals curved outward. The natural habitat for the cucumber root is the moist woods. The white, tuberous rootstock has a cucumberlike flavor; hence its common name. Its generic name honors the ancient sorceress Medea, because the plant was believed to have great curative powers.

Other plants whose flowers may appear green at some time during their development: Solomon's seal, wild sarsaparilla, and pokeweed.

W-1 TRAILING ARBUTUS     p.9

W-2 WOOD ANEMONE     p.11

W-3 RUE ANEMONE     p.9

W-4 DWARF GINSENG     p.10

W-5 BLOODROOT     p.10

W-6 DUTCHMAN'S BREECHES     p.10

22

**W-7** WHITE TRILLIUM     p.10

**W-8** SAXIFRAGE     p.11

**W-9** SPRING BEAUTY     p.11

**W-10** WILD LILY-OF-THE-VALLEY   p.11

**W-11** SOLOMON'S SEAL     p.11

**W-12** FALSE SOLOMON'S SEAL     p.12

**W-13** WILD STRAWBERRY          p. 12

**W-14** WHITE BANEBERRY          p. 12

**W-15** MAYSTAR          p. 12

**W-16** WILD SARSAPARILLA          p. 12

**W-17** DAISY          p. 13

**W-18** YARROW          p. 13

24 /

W-19 FLEABANE                    p.13     W-20 MAYAPPLE                    p.13

W-21 SPOTTED  WINTERGREEN   p.14     W-22 PARTRIDGE BERRY         p.14

W-23 QUEEN ANNE'S LACE       p.14     W-24 HORSE NETTLE            p.14

**W-25** TALL MEADOW RUE                    p.15

**W-26** MEADOWSWEET                        p.15

**W-27** PEARLY EVERLASTING                 p.15

**W-28** INDIAN PIPES                       p.15

**W-29** POKEWEED                           p.16

**W-30** ARROWHEAD                          p.16

W-31 RATTLESNAKE PLANTAIN    p.16

W-32 BONESET    p.17

W-33 WHITE WOODLAND ASTER    p.17

W-34 HEATH ASTER    p.17

W-35 TURTLEHEAD    p.17

G-1 JACK-IN-THE-PULPIT    p.18

**G-2** CUCUMBER ROOT    p.18

**R-1** RED TRILLIUM    p.19

**R-2** WILD COLUMBINE    p.19

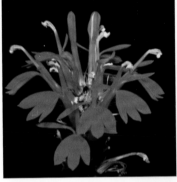

**R-3** CARDINAL FLOWER    p.19

**O-1** BUTTERFLY WEED    p.20

**O-2** WOOD LILY    p.20

**O-3** TOUCH-ME-NOT      p.20

**O-4** HAWKWEED      p.20

**Y-1** TROUT LILY      p.37

**Y-2** COLTSFOOT      p.37

**Y-3** GOLDEN RAGWORT      p.37

**Y-4** CELANDINE      p.38

**Y-5** MARSH MARIGOLD      p.38

**Y-6** CINQUEFOIL      p.38

**Y-7** DANDELION      p.39

**Y-8** GOLDSTAR GRASS      p.39

**Y-9** BUTTERCUP      p.39

**Y-10** BUTTER AND EGGS      p.39

**Y-11** BLACK-EYED SUSAN          p.40

**Y-12** YELLOW LOOSESTRIFE          p.40

**Y-13** ST. JOHNSWORT          p.40

**Y-14** COMMON MULLEIN          p.41

**Y-15** EVENING PRIMROSE          p.41

**Y-16** PARTRIDGE PEA          p.41

**Y-17** WILD LETTUCE    p.42

**Y-18** GOLDENROD    p.42

**Y-19** WILD SUNFLOWER    p.42

**B-1** BLUE-EYED GRASS    p.43

**B-2** FORGET-ME-NOT    p.43

**B-3** DAYFLOWER    p.43

**B-4** BLUE VERVAIN                    p.44    **B-5** CHICORY                    p.44

**B-6** SQUARE-STEM MONKEY FLOWER    p.44    **B-7** FRINGED GENTIAN    p.44

**Pi-1** LADY SLIPPER                    p.45    **Pi-2** STAR THISTLE                    p.45

**Pi-3** CLOVER                    p.45

**Pi-4** WILD GERANIUM           p.46

**Pi-5** DEPTFORD PINK           p.46

**Pi-6** STEEPLEBUSH             p.46

**Pi-7** MEADOW BEAUTY           p.46

**Pi-8** SMARTWEEDS              p.47

**Pi-9** TICK TREFOILS  p.47

**Pi-10** SWAMP MALLOW  p.47

**Pur-1** SKUNK CABBAGE  p.48

**Pur-2** LIVERLEAF  p.48

**Pur-3** VIOLET  p.48

**Pur-4** COW VETCH  p.49

**Pur-5** BITTERSWEET NIGHTSHADE   p.49

**Pur-6** WOOD BETONY   p.49

**Pur-7** VIRGINIA SPIDERWORT   p.49

**Pur-8** MILKWEED   p.50

**Pur-9** PURPLE MILKWORT   p.50

**Pur-10** HEAL-ALL   p.50

**Pur-11** PICKERELWEED        p.51

**Pur-12** BULL THISTLE        p.51

**Pur-13** JOE-PYE-WEED        p.51

**Pur-14** IRONWEED        p.52

**Pur-15** GREAT LOBELIA        p.52

**Pur-16** NEW ENGLAND ASTER        p.52

# 5. *Yellow Flowers*

---

**Y-1**    TROUT LILY *(Erythronium americanum)* †      Lily family
*SR*      Height: 6"–9". Flower: 1" diameter; nodding.
      Season: Early spring      (p.28)

This is a low plant growing in extensive beds in moist woods, often to the exclusion of other plants. The leaves are mottled and resemble the marks on a brook trout; hence the common name. Because of these markings and the two upright lance-shaped leaves, reminding one of alert fawn's ears, this plant is also called "fawn lily." Since several years are necessary for the production of flowers, one often finds large flowerless patches of leaves.

**Y-2**    COLTSFOOT *(Tussilago farfara)*      Composite family
*SR*      Height: 4"–6". Flower: 1" diameter.
      Season: Early spring      (p.28)

This flower, found in damp soil along ditches and streams, is often mistaken for the common dandelion, which it resembles. However, upon close inspection one finds that the flower stem is scaly and the flowers appear long before the heart-shaped leaves, which are said to resemble the shape of, and to be the size of, a colt's foot. Hence the common name.

A European immigrant, the plant was brought to this country as a cure for coughs (*tussis*, Latin for "cough"). In fact, many generations of New England children were nursed on coltsfoot-flavored candy sticks when they had a cough or cold, and the leaves were used as one of the ingredients in herbal tobacco, which was smoked as a cure for asthma.

**Y-3**    GOLDEN RAGWORT *(Senecio aureus)*      Composite family
*SR*      Height: 1'–2'. Flower: ¾" diameter.
      Season: Early spring      (p.28)

Along with the coltsfoot, this is one of the earliest composites to bloom. The flowers look like small daisies, with nine to twelve yellow petals. Although the basal leaves of the plant are heart-shaped, the stem leaves are so irregularly toothed as to give the plant a "ragged" appearance. Look for this plant in moist, open woods.

**Y-4**  CELANDINE (*Chelidonium majus*)  Poppy family
**S**  Height: 1′–2′. Flower: ½″ diameter.
  Season: Early spring  (p.28)

Another European native that has escaped cultivation, celadine is found in waste places and along roadsides. The compound leaves with numerous lobed and toothed leaflets are very conspicuous in the early spring, for this is one of the first plants to emerge. Although the small, four-petal flower does not appear until later in the spring, this plant can be easily identified by breaking a piece of the stem. The broken stem exudes a bright yellow sap that was once used as a primitive dye. The common name "celadine" is from the Greek word for "swallow," because according to the early scholars the mother swallows bathed the eyes of their young with this sap, thereby strengthening their offspring's eyesight. It was also used by herb doctors as a cure for sore eyes.

**Y-5**  MARSH MARIGOLD *(Caltha palustris)* †  Buttercup family
**SR**  Height: 8″–18″. Flower: 1″–1½″ diameter.
  Season: Early spring  (p.29)

As the common and specific names (*palustris*, Latin for "of swamps") suggest, this plant blooms in marshes and wet woods in early spring. Each flower looks like a large buttercup, and they may grow in such mass profusion that they seem to pave the marsh with gold. The very conspicuous petals are actually yellow sepals; this flower has no petals. The stems and heart-shaped leaves were once used as a cooked green vegetable, similar to spinach.

**Y-6**  CINQUEFOIL *(Potentilla spp.)*  Rose family
**S**  Height: Species variable. Flower: ½″–¾″ diameter.
  Season: Early spring  (p.29)

The edges of paths or barren fields display the shiny yellow dots of the common cinquefoil (*P. canadensis* pictured here) even before the grasses are green. There are many species of this plant, and they vary from a prostrate, creeping vine to a small shrub; but most are characterized by leaves made of five radiating leaflets; hence the common name "five fingers," which is derived from the French *cinq feuilles*, meaning "five leaves." Its habit of developing creeping runners often leads one to confuse this plant with the wild strawberry. However, the wild strawberry has white flowers and leaves made of three leaflets.

**Y-7**  DANDELION *(Taraxacum officinale)*  Composite family
*SR*  Height: 2″–6″. Flower: 1″–1½″ diameter.
  Season: Early spring  (p.29)

This ubiquitous plant springs from a large, tough root and is therefore very difficult to remove from a lawn or field, which is its preferred habitat. Although it is a scourge to the suburbanite trying to maintain a beautiful lawn, its leaves are much prized by some people as a salad green. The leaves are also responsible for its common name, which is a corruption of the French *dent de lion*, in reference to the leaf's jagged edge, resembling the teeth of a lion. The feathery, tufted seeds form downy balls, which are a delight to children and a vexation to the golfer trying to find his ball on a dandelion-infested fairway.

**Y-8**  GOLDSTAR GRASS *(Hypoxis hirsuta)*  Amaryllis family
*R*  Height: 4″–6″. Flower: ¾″ diameter.
  Season: Spring  (p.29)

The generic name of this plant tells us that its preferred habitat is acid soil *(hypoxys,* Latin for "somewhat acid") in grasslands or open woods. The leaves are grasslike and are longer than the flowering stem. Each blossom is composed of three petals and three sepals, but since they are the same color and size, the flower is a six-pointed yellow star.

**Y-9**  BUTTERCUP *(Ranunculus spp.)*  Buttercup family
*S*  Height: Species variable. Flower: ¾″–1″ diameter.
  Season: Spring  (p.29)

As its generic name suggests *(ranunculus,* Latin for "little frog"), the buttercup is usually found in a moist habitat. Although there are thirty-seven species of this plant in the United States, the buttercup is easily recognized even by children. The butter-yellow reflection of the shiny, waxy petals when the flower is held under the chin always gives an affirmative answer to the query, "Do you like butter?" However, cows are poisoned if they eat the plant.

**Y-10**  BUTTER AND EGGS *(Linaria vulgaris)*  Figwort family
*S*  Height: 8″–16″. Flower: 1″ long.
  Season: Early summer  (p.29)

A common inhabitant of waste places and roadsides, this plant was brought from Europe because it yielded a skin lotion used by the early settlers. The flowers, clustered at the top of a single stem with many narrow, bluish-green leaves, resemble the blossoms of the cultivated snapdragon. Like the snapdragon, the flower has two lips and a long spur. The "butter"-yellow flower has an orange blotch ("eggs") on its lower lip.

**Y-11**    BLACK-EYED SUSAN *(Rudbeckia serotina)*     Composite family
S       Height: 1′–3′. Flower: 3″ diameter.
       Season: Early summer                                (p.30)

Along with the daisy, this plant is a common inhabitant of the open meadows. Originally a native of the western United States, the plant was introduced into this part of the country in samples of clover seed. It is a rough plant with hairy stems and hairy, club-shaped leaves. Being a member of the composite family, it has yellow ray flowers and purplish-brown disk flowers. The disk becomes cone-shaped as it matures; hence another common name for these plants is "cone-flower."

**Y-12**    YELLOW LOOSESTRIFE *(Lysimachia terrestris)*
R       Height: 1′–3′. Flower: ⅝″ diameter.        Primrose family
       Season: Early summer                                (p.30)

The generic name of these plants honors Lysimachus, King of Sicily, who, according to tradition, used the plant to pacify an angry bull that was chasing him, i.e., he released the bull from his strife! This tradition held until fairly recent times, when the plant was fed to teams of oxen in the belief that it pacified the animals and caused them to work harmoniously together. The plant is characterized by whorls of yellow flowers with red centers, forming a slender spike. They are found in moist meadows or grassy shores.

**Y-13**    ST. JOHNSWORT *(Hypericum spp.)*     St. Johnswort family
SR      Height: 1′–3′. Flower: ¾″ diameter.
       Season: Early summer                                (p.30)

These immigrants brought with them all of the mystery and superstition that surrounded them in Europe. The plants, which were gathered on St. John's eve, June 24, were hung in the doors and windows of homes to ward off evil spirits and protect from lightning. Ointments and potions made from the plant and applied to wounds presumably led to quick healing. It was considered a potent stimulant and was used in treating depression. The more than twenty-five species found in this country soon became established in open waste fields. The fuzzy appearance of the flower is due to the numerous stamens which occupy its center. Also notice that the stemless leaves, and sometimes even the petals, have small black dots which are actually small chambers containing oil. Hold a leaf up to the sunlight and notice that these dots appear translucent.

**Y-14**    COMMON MULLEIN *(Verbascum thapus)*      Figwort family
S       Height: 2′–7′. Flower: ½″ diameter.
        Season: Early summer                             (p.30)

This biennial grows a basal rosette of large woolly leaves its first year; during the second year it produces a tall stalk with many large woolly leaves topped by a cylindrical spike containing buds, flowers, and seeds. The plant is rather unattractive, since only a few flowers appear at one time, so that the flower spike, which continues to grow all summer, carries dead flowers in addition to full and empty dry seed pods. However, this plant was much used by man. The ancient Romans dipped the dried stalks in suet and used them as torches in funeral processions, and the Greeks used the leaves as lamp wicks. The leaves, steeped as tea or mixed with tobacco to be smoked, were used as a cure for lung diseases. Indians used the leaves as inner soles in moccasins; the early settlers lined their stockings with the leaves to keep their feet warm; and even Quaker maidens, who were forbidden to use any type of makeup, used to rub their cheeks with the leaves, the slight abrasive quality causing an attractive reddening. Hail the "flannel leaf"!

**Y-15**    EVENING PRIMROSE *(Oenotheria biennis)*
S       Height: 2′–5′. Flower: 1″–1½″ diameter.      Evening-primrose family
        Season: Summer                                  (p.30)

A biennial found in dry ground in open meadows and along roadways, the evening primrose is a tall weed with narrow, pointed leaves growing alternately along the stem. The four-petal flowers found at the end of the stem usually open near sunset for one night only, new ones opening each evening. They fill the night air with the fragrance of lemons.

**Y-16**    PARTRIDGE PEA *(Cassia fasciculata)*      Bean family
S       Height: 6″–18″. Flower: 1″–1½″ diameter.
        Season: Summer                                  (p.30)

This is one of the so-called "sensitive" plants. The leaves of these plants, which consist of ten to fifteen pairs of small leaflets, fold up at night and open again in the morning sun. The plant prefers a dry, sandy soil, which is manifested by the fact that it is one of the first plants to grow in an area in which the topsoil has been removed for a gravel pit. Being a member of the bean family, it produces a rather conspicuous seed pod containing seeds which are relished by gamebirds.

**Y-17**   WILD LETTUCE *(Lactuca spp.)*                Composite family
S       Height: 3′–10′. Flower: ⅜″ diameter.
        Season: Late summer                                      (p.31)

Although the flowers of this plant are quite small and inconspicuous, the great height of many of these plants form a conspicuous part of wet and open thickets during the late summer. If at a distance you see a tall plant with large, deeply lobed, lance-shaped leaves topped with a large number of conspicuous fuzzy balls, actually a collection of feathery, tufted seeds, you have found a wild lettuce. On close inspection you will find small yellow or blue flowers. If you remove a leaf, you will notice that the stem "bleeds" a milky juice, which accounts for its generic name *(lac,* Latin for "milk").

**Y-18**   GOLDENROD *(Solidago spp.)*                 Composite family
SR      Height: 2′–4′. Flower:⅛″-¼″ long; variously shaped clusters.
        Season: Late summer                                      (p.31)

In the late summer and early fall the meadows and roadsides glow with the radiant yellows of the tiny flowers that make up the flower heads of goldenrod. Everyone recognizes goldenrod, with its alternate leaves, but species identification is difficult, since there are at least 75 species of this plant, more than 40 species being found in the northeast. This plant has gained some notoriety through the years. Its beauty has earned it a place as the state flower of Alabama, Kentucky, and Nebraska. Its reputed healing powers are responsible for its generic designation, since *solidus* is Latin for "whole," in other words, "to make whole." It has been vilified as a causative agent in hay fever, although recent evidence indicates that the pollen of goldenrod is too heavy to be windborne; it is actually the inconspicuous flowers of the ragweed, which blooms at the same time as goldenrod, that are the principal culprit during the fall "sneeze season."

**Y-19**   WILD SUNFLOWER *(Helianthus spp.)*          Composite family
S       Height: 3′–12′. Flower: 2½″–3″ diameter.
        Season: Late summer                                      (p.31)

There are approximately one hundred species of sunflower. The generic name is a combination of two Greek words—*helios* ("sun") and *anthos* ("flower"). The early Incas worshiped this flower as a symbol of the sun. The plant is found in wet meadows and moist ground, where the yellow-rayed flowers are displayed conspicuously on tall stems. The leaves of most sunflowers are characterized by two prominent veins coming from the midrib near its base. Wild sunflower seeds provide valuable nutrients for various kinds of animal life.

Other flowers, certain species or varieties of which may appear yellow: violet, hawkweeds, clover, and wood betony.

# 6. Blue Flowers

---

**B-1**    BLUE-EYED GRASS *(Sisyrinchium spp.)*                    Iris family
*SR*       Height: 6″–12″. Flower: ½″–¾″ diameter.
           Season: Early summer                                              (p.31)

This delicate flower is a rather subdued member of the flamboyant iris family.
It is found in moist meadows and open fields, where its dark-green, grasslike
leaves blend in with the other grasses present. The starlike flower is composed
of three petals and three petal-like sepals, all of which end in a pointed tip. These
flowers last only one day and open only in bright sunlight.

**B-2**    FORGET-ME-NOT *(Myosotis scorpioides)*                  Borage family
*SC*       Height: Sprawling 12″–18″. Flower: ⅓″ diameter.
           Season: Early summer                                              (p.31)

A symbol of love, this perennial of European origin is found along the swampy
margins of streams and in wet meadows. The common name comes from an
incident in German folk history, in which a knight who was drowning in a
stream tossed a sprig of this plant to his distraught lover, who was helplessly
standing on the bank, crying, "Forget me not." Although the plant can grow
to one and one-half feet in length, it is usually seen as a sprawling, tangled mass
of lance-shaped leaves. The specific name, *scorpioides* (Latin for "scorpionlike"),
refers to the flower stems, which are curved around like the tail of a scorpion.

**B-3**    DAYFLOWER *(Commelina communis)*                    Spiderwort family
*SRC*      Height: Sprawling 1′–2′. Flower: ½″ diameter.
           Season: Early summer                                              (p.31)

Like its close relative the spiderwort, the dayflower blooms only a few hours
before dying, and then only on warm, sunny days. A native of Asia, this plant
escaped cultivation and now grows successfully in cool woods or along the banks
of streams. The bases of its lance-shaped leaves clasp the jointed stem of this
sprawling perennial. The flower, with its two prominent blue petals and one
small, inconspicuous, faded petal, is responsible for the generic name of this
plant. Linnaeus, the famous plant taxonomist, dedicated the plant to the three
Commelin brothers: two were notable botanists, and the third "died before
accomplishing anything in botany."

**B-4**    BLUE VERVAIN *(Verbena hastata)*                Verbena family
*SRC*    Height: 4'-6'. Flower: ¼" diameter; few on a slender spike.
         Season: Summer                                            (p.32)

These plants, with pairs of toothed, lance-shaped leaves along their tall stems, are found along ponds and lakes and in damp, open woods. The thin flower spikes are never in full bloom; only a small ring of tiny blossoms is open at any one time. The generic name *Verbena* is the Latin name for any sacred herb. Because of this reputation, it was much sought after by herb doctors.

**B-5**    CHICORY *(Cichorium intybus)*                Composite family
*S*      Height: 1'-3'. Flower: 1½"-2".
         Season: Summer                                            (p.32)

This handsome flower but noxious weed is found along roadsides and in waste places. The basal rosette of leaves eventually gives rise to rank stems with small, lance-shaped leaves. The flowers open at sunrise and close by noon and seldom open at all if the day is cloudy. The plant was brought to this country from Europe, where its dried and ground root was used to improve the flavor of coffee.

**B-6**    SQUARE-STEM MONKEY FLOWER·*(Mimulus ringens)*
*SRC*    Height: 1'-3'. Flower: ½"-¾" diameter.                Figwort family
         Season: Summer                                            (p.32)

Taxonomists saw a resemblance between this grinning, flop-eared flower and the head of a monkey, the natural buffoon (*mimus*, Latin for "buffoon"). The square stems (feel them!) have pairs of opposite, coarsely toothed, lance-shaped leaves. The flowers arise from the stem, where the upper leaves meet the stem. Look for this plant along the banks of streams and in swamps and wet fields.

**B-7**    FRINGED GENTIAN *(Gentiana crinita)* †                Gentian family
*S*      Height: 6"-12". Flower: 1"-2" length.
         Season: Fall                                              (p.32)

When almost all the other flowers have died and gone to seed, the beautiful gentian begins to bloom and continues to produce flowers until the first heavy frost. The stems, with opposite, oval leaves, are topped with dark-blue flowers composed of four fringed petals. Its natural habitat is cool, damp thickets and meadows. The roots of some species of this plant once had medicinal value. This was discovered by Gentius, King of Illyria, an ancient country along the Adriatic Sea, hence the common and generic name.

Other flowers, certain species or varieties of which may appear blue: wild lettuce, liverleaf, cow vetch, great lobelia, and fleabane.

# 7. Pink Flowers

---

**Pi-1**    LADY SLIPPER *(Cypripedium acuale)* †          Orchid family
**R**       Height: 8″–12″. Flower: 2″ long.
        Season: Spring                                            (p.32)
The bleakness of the woods and bogs in which this plant grows accentuates its elegant beauty. The showy pink flower emerges between two hairy, basal leaves. The "slipper" is a saclike petal with a longitudinal cleft. If an insect lands on this cleft it drops into the sac, and the only way out is through the two openings at the rear of the "slipper." But in passing through these openings the insect brushes against the reproductive organs located here, thus ensuring pollination. Look for this flower off the beaten path, since ruthless picking has made it a rarity in areas traversed by many people.

**Pi-2**    STAR THISTLE *(Centaurea cyanus)*          Composite family
**S**       Height: 2′–4′. Flower: 1½″–2″ diameter.
        Season: Spring                                            (p.32)
This thornless thistle is a European import that has escaped cultivation. It is a bushy-appearing plant with small, oblong leaves and is usually found along roadsides and in open meadows, where it blooms continuously until late summer. Another common name for this plant is "bachelor's button," which refers to the charming practice of a bygone era when English maidens wore the flower as a sign that they were eligible for marriage.

**Pi-3**    CLOVER *(Trifolium spp.)*                 Bean family
**S**       Height: 8″–15″. Flower: ⅜″ long; many in a globular head.
        Season: Spring                                            (p.33)
The common clover is a rather uncommon plant. The generic name refers to the characteristic three oblong leaflets that go to make up the leaf, which some people claim is the true shamrock of Ireland. The plant, which produces flowers of various colors, not only adds beauty to the lawns and meadows in which it grows; its root system harbors nitrogen-fixing bacteria, which add nutrients to the soil. The word "clover" is derived from the Latin *clava*, meaning "clubs." This is in reference to the three-knobbed club of Hercules, which the leaves were thought to resemble. The next time you play cards, take a close look at the symbol for clubs.

**Pi-4**   WILD GERANIUM *(Geranium maculatum)* †   Geranium family
SR   Height: 1′–2′. Flower: 1″–1½″ diameter.
  Season: Spring   (p.33)

A patch of wild geranium adds a bright spot to an otherwise bleak, sparsely leafed, spring woodland. The soft-pink flowers and broad, finely cut leaves give the plant a delicate appearance in the coarse surroundings. The shape of the seed pod is responsible for the common and generic names of this plant, since it is said to resemble the beak of a crane (*geranos*, Greek for "crane").

**Pi-5**   DEPTFORD PINK *(Dianthus armeria)*   Pink family
S   Height: 8″–24″. Flower: ½″ diameter.
  Season: Early summer   (p.33)

What could Jupiter (*Dianthus*, Greek for "Jupiter's flower") have seen in this grasslike plant with small leaves and fairly inconspicuous flowers growing along roadsides and dry places? Close inspection reveals a delicate pink flower mottled with white dots and having "pinked" petals—a wise choice by the chief of the Roman gods. The common name refers to its European origin, since it once grew in abundance in Deptford, England.

**Pi-6**   STEEPLEBUSH *(Spiraea tomentosa)*   Rose family
R   Height: 2′–4′. Flower: ¼″ diameter; spikelike cluster.
  Season: Summer   (p.33)

Steeplebush is found in moist meadows and wooded fields along with its close relative the meadowsweet. It can be distinguished from meadowsweet by the spirelike arrangement of its pink blossoms and its ovate leaves with very hairy undersurfaces. The undersurfaces of these leaves are so woolly that they are responsible for the specific name *tomentose*, Latin for "cushion stuffing."

**Pi-7**   MEADOW BEAUTY *(Rhexia virginica)*   Melastoma family
SR   Height: 1′–2′. Flower: 1″ diameter.
  Season: Summer   (p.33)

The meadow beauty is a fugitive from the tropics. The Melastoma family is almost entirely tropical, with the exception of *Rhexia*. The flower is unique because of its unusually long and curved yellow anthers. The plant grows in moist, sandy, open woods or meadows, where the brilliant pink flowers sparkle from the tops of square stems with stemless, opposite, oval leaves. Because it is relished as food by deer, it is also called "deergrass."

**Pi-8**  SMARTWEEDS *(Polygonum spp.)*                Buckwheat family
S      Height: Variable. Flower: ⅛″–³⁄₁₆″ diameter; many in spikelike cluster.
       Season: Summer                                           (p.33)

There are a great many species of this ubiquitous plant. Many species are found near or in water. Most species have pink flowers, but some may bear white blossoms. One group has curved prickles on its stems and is called "tearthumbs." Another common name, "knotweeds," is derived from the generic name (*poly*, Latin for "many"; *gonu*, Latin for "joint" or "knee"), which refers to the many swollen joints that are characteristic of the stems of these plants. Another characteristic is the presence of a sheath at the junction of the leaf with the stem. The spikelike cluster of flowers eventually gives rise to seeds relished as food by gamebirds.

**Pi-9**  TICK TREFOILS *(Desmodium spp.)*                  Bean family
S      Height: 2′–5′. Flower: ½″–¾″ length.
       Season: Summer                                           (p.34)

We might not pay any attention to this rank weed except that during the late summer and the fall a walk through the open woods usually ends with time being spent removing the small, roughly triangular seed pods from clothing. The seed pods, which are connected in groups containing two to five units (*desmos*, Greek for "chain"), have hooked bristles which easily catch and cling to clothing and animal hair. There are many species of this plant which in addition to having the unique seed pods are also characterized by small pealike flowers and compound leaves composed of three leaflets (trefoil).

**Pi-10**  SWAMP MALLOW *(Hibiscus palustris)*              Mallow family
SRC    Height: 4′–6′. Flower: 6″ diameter.
       Season: Late summer                                      (p.34)

The mallows can be easily recognized by the peculiar structure in the center of the flower—many stamens projecting from a central stalk like the bristles in a bottle brush. The swamp, or rose, mallow has tall canelike stems with pointed, ovate leaves. The delicate though large flowers of this plant seem out of place in the hostile environment of a swamp or marsh. The root of one of the European members of this family was the original source of the material that was used to make the favorite campfire confection—marshmallows.

Other flowers, certain species or varieties of which may appear pink: spring beauty, white trillium, fleabanes, trailing arbutus, turtlehead, cow vetch, and milkwort.

# 8. *Purple Flowers*

---

**Pur-1** SKUNK CABBAGE *(Symplocarpus foetidus)* Arum family
S Height: 4″–6″. Flower: tiny, in a knoblike spike surrounded by a spathe.
Season: Early spring (p.34)

The traditional heralds of spring, these are the first flowers to emerge; in fact, they may have started the previous fall. It is not unusual to walk in the woods following a snowstorm in February or March and see the flower of skunk cabbage poking through the snow. These plants are found in depressions and hollows in the open woods wherever there is an abundance of soil water. The small inconspicuous flowers are arranged on a knoblike spike enclosed within a yellow-dappled, dark-purple, hoodlike spathe. Breaking the spathe or leaves gives the characteristic skunk odor (*foetidus*, Latin for "foul-smelling").

**Pur-2** LIVERLEAF *(Hepatica americana)* † Buttercup family
SR Height: 4″–6″. Flower: ½″ diameter.
Season: Early spring (p.34)

Another, almost incongruous herald of spring is the delicate flower of the liver-leaf. Toward the end of March, the fragile-looking flowers with their conspicuous petal-like sepals push their way up through the debris that covers the wooded slopes on which they are found. The new leaves appear later in the spring. The shape of the leaf is the reason for the common and generic names of this plant. It was thought to resemble the three-lobed mammalian liver (*hepaticus*, Latin for "pertaining to the liver"). Herb doctors who practiced their art according to the "doctrine of signatures" used this plant to treat liver ailments.

**Pur-3** VIOLET *(Viola spp.)* Violet family
SR Height: 4″–6″. Flower: ¾″–1¼″ diameter.
Season: Early spring (p.34)

Another flower closely associated with the early spring is the violet. There are many species of violet, and most are found in rich open woods or the edge of meadows. Although the purple meadow violets are conspicuous by their size and numbers, the earliest violet to bloom in the spring is a small yellow violet of the woodlands. Many violets produce showy sterile flowers, the fertile ones being closed, self-pollinating, inconspicuous, budlike flowers found at the base of the plant. Cut-up violet flowers are used by some people as a decorative garnish on salads, where they not only provide color but also are a concentrated source of vitamin C.

**Pur-4** COW VETCH *(Vicia cracca)* Bean family
S Height: Climbing. Flower: ½″ long.
Season: Spring (p.34)

A common inhabitant of waste places and fields, this plant was brought to this country from Europe as a forage crop for cattle. It grows in patches, the dark-green leaves composed of eight to twelve pairs of leaflets and the hanging clusters of purple flowers calling it to our attention. It has often been plowed under as a "green manure," since its roots contain nitrogen-fixing bacteria which produce nitrates, a valuable plant nutrient.

**Pur-5** BITTERSWEET NIGHTSHADE *(Solanum dulcamara)*
S Height: Climbing vine. Flower: ½″ diameter. Nightshade family
Season: Spring (p.35)

Another European import that has invaded thickets and fence rows is the bitter-sweet nightshade. The vine is rather handsome—ovate, alternate leaves with two conspicuous lobes at their bases, and a cone of yellow stamens in the center of the purple star-shaped flower. However, the leaves of this plant are poisonous, as is the fruit. The common name is attributable to a report by early botanists that the chewed root first tasted bitter, then sweet.

**Pur-6** WOOD BETONY *(Pedicularis canadensis)* Figwort family
S Height: 6″–10″. Flower: ¾″ long.
Season: Spring (p.35)

Even though it doesn't bloom until May, this plant is often conspicuous in April because of its rosette of very unusual fernlike leaves. The purple or yellow flowers are found in clusters at the top of a common stalk. A popular name for this plant is "lousewort," from the European belief that cattle that grazed near them became infested with lice. The generic name also reflects this belief (*pedicularis*, Latin for "louse"). Look for these plants in open woods and clearings.

**Pur-7** VIRGINIA SPIDERWORT *(Tradescantia virginiana)*
SRC Height: 1′–2′. Flower: 1″–1½″ diameter. Spiderwort family
Season: Spring (p.35)

Morning is the only time to look for this flower, since it usually closes by noon. The flowers are interspersed throughout the masses of long, tapering, grasslike leaves, whose angular growth suggests spider legs. The center of the three-petal flower also contains long filaments covered with fuzzy hair, again suggesting a spider; hence the common name. The plant prefers partial shade and is found in thickets and open woods and meadows. The generic name honors John Trades-cant, a botanist and gardener to Charles I of England.

**Pur-8** MILKWEED *(Asclepias spp.)* Milkweed family
SR  Height: 3'–5'. Flower: ½" diameter; spherical cluster.
Season: Early summer (p.35)

There are about twenty-five species of milkweeds in the eastern United States, most of which bear flowers that are some shade of purple or red. In general the plants are characterized by leaves that are usually oval or lance-shaped, arranged in pairs along a stem that bleeds a milky sap when broken. Habitat varies with species from dry, open places to swamps, where you find the swamp milkweed *(A. incarnata)*, illustrated here. During the fall the seed pod of the plants commands our attention because of its seeds with long, silky hairs. Early settlers in this country used this hair to stuff pillows and mattresses, and during World War I children were paid a penny a pound for milkweed "silk," to be used to stuff life preservers when the regular material used was no longer available.

**Pur-9** PURPLE MILKWORT *(Polygala sanguinea)* Milkwort family
S  Height: 6"–12". Flower: ¼" long; oval cluster.
Season: Early summer (p.35)

This small annual is found in moist meadows in acid soil, where its flower is often mistaken for clover. However, close inspection will reveal not the typical cloverleaf but small, narrow leaves. The common name refers not to a milky sap but to the ancient belief that dairy cattle fed this plant increased their flow of milk. This belief is reflected in the Greek derivation of its generic name *polys*, meaning "much"; and *gala*, meaning "milk." The plant is also called "candyroot" because the crushed root has a wintergreen flavor.

**Pur-10** HEAL-ALL *(Prunella vulgaris)* Mint family
SR  Height: 4"–8". Flower: ½" long; many on a blunt spike.
Season: Summer (p.35)

Another European plant brought to this country by the early herb doctors was the heal-all. It had an outstanding reputation in Europe as a medicinal herb. It was applied to all types of wounds in England, and the French had a proverb which said that if one had heal-all one had no need for a surgeon. The generic name is a corruption of the German word *Brunelle*, which means "quinsy," a type of fever that was supposed to be cured by the herb. Being a member of the mint family, the plant has the typical square stem with opposite, oval leaves. It can be found along roadsides and in fields.

**Pur-11** PICKERELWEED *(Pontederia cordata)*        Pickerelweed family
R        Height: 1′–2′. Flower: ⅜″ long; many on a spike.
        Season: Summer                                              (p.36)

This plant grows in the shallow, quiet waters of lakes, streams, and ponds favored by pickerel; hence its common name. The flower stalk and single heart-shaped leaf (*chorda*, Latin for "heart") sometimes form an almost impenetrable barrier above the surface of the water, which is a bane to boatmen and fishermen who try to use these waters. However, the flowers produce seeds in the fall that serve as food for wild ducks.

**Pur-12** BULL THISTLE *(Cirsium vulgare)*              Composite family
S        Height: 3′–5′. Flower: 2″–3″ diameter.
        Season: Summer                                              (p.36)

When one looks at a thistle, one thinks, "Pins and needles." The stems, lobed leaves, and even the flowers of this biennial plant contain sharp prickles. The common bull thistle is of European origin and quickly spread in this country, where it is found in meadows, waste places, and along roadsides. The plumed seeds, which appear in late summer and fall, are relished as food by the goldfinch.

This plant was used by herb doctors, who believed in the "doctrine of signatures." If you look at the underside of the leaves of these plants you will notice that the vein in the midline is bulged along its entire length. Some herb doctors saw this as a varicose vein and used the plant for treating this condition. This practice is reflected in its generic name *cirsos*, Greek for "swollen vein."

**Pur-13** JOE-PYE-WEED *(Eupatorium maculatum)*        Composite family
S        Height: 3′–5′. Flower: ½″ long; many in a flat head.
        Season: Late summer                                         (p.36)

The heralds of fall are the yellow of the goldenrod and the purple wine-stain color of the Joe-Pye-weed. This tall plant with whorled, coarsely toothed, oval leaves grows in wet meadows and roadside ditches. The flowers are so similar to those of boneset in both size and shape that this plant is often called "purple boneset." The reputed healing powers of this plant are also legend. The generic name honors the herb doctor Eupator, who used this plant during biblical times. During colonial times in New England an Indian herb doctor called Joe Pye was said to have used this plant to stem a typhus-fever epidemic in Massachusetts.

**Pur-14** IRONWEED *(Veronia noveboracensis)* Composite family
SRC Height: 4′–6′. Flower: 1″–1½″ diameter; several in open, flat cluster.
Season: Late summer (p.36)

This plant appears at the same time and same places as the Joe-Pye-weed, but they can never be confused because of the difference in coloration of the flowers. Ironweed is a deep purple, in contrast to the dull wine-stain color of Joe-Pye-weed. This is not evident in most color pictures, because ironweed photographs a dark pink with most types of film used. Look for this tall plant with alternate, narrow, finely toothed leaves in damp thickets and meadows.

**Pur-15** GREAT LOBELIA *(Lobelia syphilitica)* Lobelia family
SRC Height: 1′–3′. Flower: 1″ long; many in a spike.
Season: Late summer (p.36)

This lobelia, in contrast to its much more flamboyant relative, the cardinal flower, is not seen as readily because of its subdued color and its habit of growing with other plants that may be as tall as or taller than it. This secretive plant, with its alternate, lance-shaped leaves tapering at both ends, grows in wet meadows and along the banks of streams. The specific name is due to the belief that the roots of this plant could be used as a treatment for syphilis.

**Pur-16** NEW ENGLAND ASTER *(Aster novae-angliae)* Composite family
S Height: 4′–8′. Flower: 1½″–2″ diameter.
Season: Late summer (p.36)

There are many species of aster which produce flowers with various hues of purple. The most conspicuous and certainly the most beautiful one found in the northeast is the New England aster. It is usually found in wet meadows or swampy places. The tall stems, with stalkless, lance-shaped leaves, are topped by flowers composed of deep-purple ray flowers and brilliant orange-yellow disk flowers. It is surprising that this magnificent wild flower was not adopted by any of the New England states as its state flower.

Other flowers, certain species or varieties of which may appear purple: star thistle, clover, blue vervain, blue-eyed grass, and smartweed.

# Similar Plants

(The number codes below refer to plant descriptions on pages 9–52.)

**W-1**    Massachusetts has adopted this plant as the state flower.

**W-6**    A similar species with a more heart-shaped flower with round spurs is Squirrel-corn (*D. canadensis*). The common name is derived from the small, yellow tubers that occur on its rootstock and bear a fancied resemblance to grains of corn.

**W-7**    Nodding Trillium (*T. cernuum*) is also a white-flowered species, but as its common name suggests the flower hangs downward beneath the leaves. The flower of Painted Trillium (*T. undulatum*) is smaller (2″–2½″) and its center is streaked ("painted") with red.

**W-9**    A similar species, Carolina Spring Beauty (*C. caroliniana*), has wide leaves. The genus is named for John Clayton, an early American botanist.

**W-11**    A larger (over 4′ tall) species, Great Solomon's Seal (*P. canaliculatum*), has flowers that hang in clusters of 2–10 blossoms.

**W-12**    A shorter (less than 2′) species, Starry False Solomon's Seal (*S. stellata*), has larger starry flowers.

**W-13**    The Wood Strawberry (*F. vesca*) is very similar except that its berry is cone-shaped and is rather dry and tasteless.

**W-14**    Although very similar, the Red Baneberry (*A. rubra*) usually produces red, glossy berries.

**W-17**    A shorter (8″–20″), but similar, plant is Mayweed (*Anthemis cotula*). It is easily distinguished from a daisy because of its very disagreeable odor. Care should be exercised if the plant is picked, because its acrid juice can raise blisters.

**W-21**    A similar species also called Pipsissewa (*C. umbellata*) has pink or flesh-colored flowers and its leaves are without white stripes. Fresh leaves are refreshing when chewed.

**W-23**    A larger (2′–6′) plant with similar-appearing flowers and leaves, but with purple streaks on the stem, is Poison Hemlock (*Conium maculatum*). All parts of the plant are extremely toxic if eaten and cause paralysis and death. An extract of this plant was used by ancient Greeks as a method of executing criminals. Another poisonous plant, Fool's Parsley (*Aethusa cynopium*), closely resembles Queen Anne's Lace, but it has conspicuous green, tri-forked structures hanging down underneath each small cluster of flowers that make up the flat flower head. It also has shiny leaves that resemble those of parsley, but they are poisonous; hence the common name.

**W-28** Although the single flower of Indian Pipe is usually white, occasionally one finds a pink specimen. However, if the plant has several nodding pink or dull yellow flowers it is Pinesap (*M. hypopithys*).

**W-30** Growing in the bogs and swamps along the coast of Massachusetts are three additional species with characteristic flowers but differing in their leaf shapes. Grass-leaved Arrowhead (*S. graminea*) has linear leaves. Slender Arrowhead (*S. teres*) has cylindrical, pointed leaves. Engelmann's Arrowhead (*S. engelmanniana*) has very slender, arrow-shaped leaves.

**W-31** The flowers of Checkered Rattlesnake Plantain (*G. tesselata*) are arranged in a spiral along the stem. The leaves of Green-leaved Rattlesnake Plantain (*G. oblongifolia*) may have a white midvein but lack the network of white lines.

**W-32** A similar species whose leaves are heart-shaped and stalked and is found blooming in the woods is White Snakeroot (*E. rugosum*). As its common name suggests it was once used to treat snakebite.

**O-2** A similar-appearing lily but with its flower (or flowers) hanging downward is Canada Lily (*L. canadense*). Although orange is the more common form, there are also red and yellow forms.

**O-3** A less common yellow species, *I. pallida*, has a flower with a downward pointing spur.

**Y-3** During the late summer the Tansy Ragwort (*S. jacobaea*) is found in several areas of Massachusetts. It is identified by its finely cut leaves. It was brought here from Europe where it was called Stinking Willie. This name was given to it by the Scots who made known their feelings when they were defeated in battle by the army of the English nobleman, William, Duke of Cumberland. The English, on the other hand, named a different flower Sweet William to commemorate their victory.

**Y-7** Dwarf Dandelion (*Krigia virginica*), a single-flowered plant with dandelionlike leaves, is also common throughout Massachusetts. Also the Red-seeded Dandelion (*T. erythrospermum*) is easily identified by its red seeds and very deeply toothed leaves.

**Y-11**   In the Green-headed Coneflower the disk is green and the petals appear to be slightly droopy. If the disk is deep purplish and the petals have three lobes at their tips, this is the Purple-headed Sneezeweed (*Helenium nudiflorum*), a plant once used as an ingredient in snuff; hence its common name.

**Y-12**   The Whorled Loosestrife (*L. quadrifolia*) has whorls of flowers arising from whorls of lance-shaped leaves at regular intervals along the stem. The Fringed Loosestrife (*L. ciliata*) has nodding flowers arising from pairs of leaves, which have fringed leafstalks.

**Y-15**   A shorter (1'–3'), but similar, plant that is day-blooming is Sundrops (*O. fruticosa*).

**B-7**   A deep blue species whose petals never open is the Closed Gentian (*G. andrewsii*).

**Pi-1**   The Yellow Lady Slipper (*C. calceolus*) has a yellow "slipper." A large showy plant whose "slipper" is white streaked with pink or purple and surrounded by white petals is the Showy Lady Slipper (*C. reginae*).

**Pi-4**   A small-flowered species (½" diameter) with flowers crowded into clusters is Carolina Cranesbill (*G. carolinianum*). Another species with small flowers occurring singly or in pairs and having fernlike leaves is Herb Robert (*G. robertianum*). It is dedicated to St. Robert, hence its common name.

**Pi-5**   A similar species having solitary flowers with larger, rounder petals is Maiden Pink (*D. deltoides*).

**Pur-8**   A most ubiquitous milkweed that is found along roadsides and in areas of dry soil is the Common Milkweed (*A. syriaca*). Its flowers, which vary in color from rose to brownish purple, are arranged in a domed cluster of drooping flowers, and the plant is covered with a fine down. However, if the leaves have clasping bases and their edges are wavy, this identifies the Blunt-leaved Milkweed (*A. amplexicaulis*). Whorls of four leaves along the stem identifies the Four-leaved Milkweed (*A. quadrifolia*).

**Pur-9**   Growing in the sandy soil and bogs along the coast of Massachusetts is found the Cross-leaved Milkwort (*P. cruciata*). Its narrow leaves are arranged in whorls of four (forming a cross) along the stem; hence, the common name.

**Pur-12**   The Pasture Thistle (*C. pumilum*) is very similar to *C. vulgare* but can easily be identified because it has a hairy stem, whereas Bull Thistle has prickly "wings" on the stem.

**Pur-13**   *E. maculatum* has purple stems, but Sweet Joe-Pye-weed (*E. purpurem*) has green stems and its leaves emit the odor of vanilla when crushed.

# *Appendix*

## EARLY SPRING March–early May

**White**
Trailing Arbutus
Rue Anemone
Wood Anemone
Dwarf Ginseng
Bloodroot
Dutchman's Breeches
Saxifrage
Spring Beauty

**Yellow**
Trout Lily
Coltsfoot
Golden Ragwort
Marsh Marigold
Cinquefoil
Dandelion

**Purple**
Skunk Cabbage
Violet
Liverleaf

## SPRING May–mid-June

**White**
Wild Lily-of-the-valley
Solomon's Seal
False Solomon's Seal
Wild Strawberry
Maystar
Wild Sarsaparilla
Daisy
Yarrow
Fleabane
Mayapple
White Trillium
White Baneberry

**Green**
Jack-in-the-pulpit
Cucumber Root

**Red**
Wild Columbine
Red Trillium

**Yellow**
Butter and Eggs
Celandine
Goldstar Grass
Buttercup

**Pink**
Lady Slipper
Star Thistle
Clover
Wild Geranium

**Purple**
Cow Vetch
Bittersweet Nightshade
Wood Betony
Virginia Spiderwort

## EARLY SUMMER mid-June–mid-July

**White**
Spotted Wintergreen
Partridge Berry
Queen Anne's Lace
Horse Nettle

**Orange**
Touch-me-not
Hawkweed

**Yellow**
Black-eyed Susan
Yellow Loosestrife
St. Johnswort
Common Mullein

**Blue**
Blue-eyed Grass
Forget-me-not
Dayflower

**Pink**
Deptford Pink

**Purple**
Milkweed
Purple Milkwort
Heal-all

## SUMMER mid-July–August

**White**
Meadowsweet
Boneset
Pearly Everlasting
Indian Pipes
Arrowhead
Rattlesnake Plantain
Tall Meadow Rue
Pokeweed

**Orange**
Butterfly Weed
Wood Lily

**Yellow**
Evening Primrose
Partridge Pea

**Blue**
Blue Vervain
Square-stem
 Monkey Flower
Chicory

**Pink**
Meadow Beauty
Steeplebush
Smartweeds
Tick Trefoils

**Purple**
Pickerelweed
Bull Thistle

## LATE SUMMER August–September

**White**
White Woodland Aster
Heath Aster
Turtlehead

**Red**
Cardinal Flower

**Yellow**
Wild Sunflower
Goldenrod
Wild Lettuce

**Pink**
Swamp Mallow

**Purple**
Joe-Pye-weed
Ironweed
Great Lobelia
New England Aster

## FALL mid-September–October

**Blue**
Fringed Gentian

# Index of Common Names

*The first page reference is for text; the second is for illustration.*

# Index of Scientific Names

*The first page reference is for text; the second is for illustration.*